D0895641

Fact Finders®

GREAT CIVILIZATIONS

ANCIENT ROME

A MIGHTY EMPIRE

by Muriel L. Dubois

CAPSTONE PRESS
a capstone imprint

Fact Finders are published by Capstone Press,
1710 Roe Crest Drive, North Mankato, Minnesota 56003.
www.capstonepub.com

Books published by Capstone Press are manufactured with paper
containing at least 10 percent post-consumer waste.

Library of Congress Cataloging-in-Publication Data
Dubois, Muriel L.
 Ancient Rome : a mighty empire / by Muriel L. Dubois.
  p. cm.—(Fact finders. Great civilizations)
 Summary: "Describes ancient Rome, including its earliest inhabitants, government structure, major
achievements, and rise to power, as well as its lasting influences on the world"—Provided by publisher.
 Includes bibliographical references and index.
 ISBN 978-1-4296-6832-3 (library binding)
 ISBN 978-1-4296-7239-9 (paperback)
 1. Rome—Civilization—Juvenile literature. 2. Civilization, Modern—Roman influences—Juvenile
literature. I. Title. II. Series.
 DG77.D793 2012
 937—dc22   2011002114

Editorial Credits
Carrie Braulick Sheely and Jennifer Besel, editors; Lori Bye, designer; Svetlana Zhurkin, media
        researcher; Eric Manske, production specialist

Photo Credits
Alamy: Interfoto, 9, 14, 24; The Bridgeman Art Library: Private Collection/Look and Learn, 5, 21;
Corbis: Bettmann, 13; Dreamstime: R. Gino Santa Maria, 28 and 29 (border); Getty Images: DEA/A. de
Gregorio, 19 (right), The Bridgeman Art Library, 18; iStockphoto: David Evans, cover and 1 (statue),
David MacFarlane, cover and 1 (column), Fabio Bianchini, 11, Giorgio Fochesato (Latin inscription used
as background), Grafissimo, 22, Lauri Wiberg, 27 (clock), ZU_09, 23; Mary Evans Picture Library, 17;
Shutterstock: Csaba Peterdi, 16, Elena Elisseeva, 25, Konstantin L., 26, magicinfoto (light beige texture
paper design), Malgorzata Kistryn, 10, Marilyn Volan (grunge paper design), Paul Picone, cover and 1
(coin), Petrov Stanislav Eudardovich (parchment paper design), pjcross, 27, pseudolongino, 15, Ronald
Sumners, cover (back), 1 (back), vectorkat, back cover (coin); Wikimedia/Jebulon, 19 (left)

Printed in the United States of America in North Mankato, Minnesota.
042013   007258R

TABLE OF CONTENTS

CHAPTER 1

THE GREAT CONQUERORS

The Roman army descended upon the city of Carthage in northern Africa in 146 BC. Soldiers battled fiercely. Arrows soared through the air. The armies had been fighting for the past three years. The people of Carthage had broken a peace treaty. Rome wasn't going to let them get away with it.

This war wasn't the first time the two armies had battled. They had fought two other wars in the last 100 years. Both times, the armies had been battling over land. And both times the Roman army won.

This final war would be no different. Rome had more soldiers and resources. They defeated their enemies and destroyed Carthage. The victories of the **Punic** Wars made Rome one of the most powerful nations in the ancient world.

Punic: the Latin word for Phoenician that was used to describe the wars between Rome and Carthage

Carthage was completely destroyed by the Romans during the Third Punic War.

FACT: The First Punic War lasted for 23 years. The Second Punic War lasted for 17 years. The third lasted just three years.

The Greatness of Rome

Rome began as a **city-state** in Italy in about 753 BC. For the next 1,200 years, Romans conquered other groups of people. Eventually, the Roman civilization became the strongest in the world.

The ancient Romans had two great strengths. They had well-organized, powerful armies. Roman soldiers, carrying heavy armor, traveled long distances in one day. The Roman army stayed to guard conquered territories. The soldiers built roads, bridges, and forts.

Rome's second strength was the ability to adopt ideas from the people it conquered. Romans copied the inventions, art, and religion of other people. Romans improved their own culture with the best of outside customs.

When Rome was strongest, the **empire** surrounded the Mediterranean Sea. At least 30 present-day countries were once part of Rome.

city-state: a self-governing community including a town and its surrounding territory
empire: a large territory ruled by a powerful leader

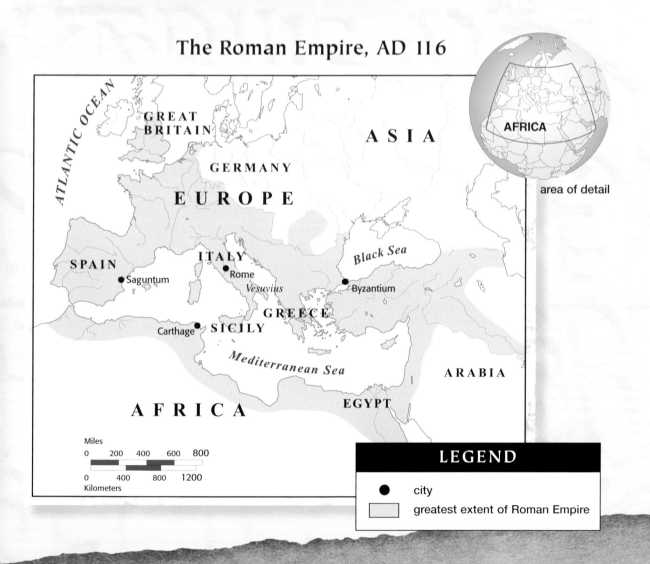

The Roman Empire, AD 116

ATLANTIC OCEAN

GREAT BRITAIN

ASIA

GERMANY

EUROPE

SPAIN

• Saguntum

ITALY

• Rome

Vesuvius

Black Sea

• Byzantium

GREECE

SICILY

Carthage •

Mediterranean Sea

ARABIA

AFRICA

EGYPT

Miles
0   200   400   600   800

0   400   800   1200
Kilometers

AFRICA

area of detail

LEGEND

● city

☐ greatest extent of Roman Empire

Livy's Books

Much of what we know about ancient Rome comes from Titus Livius, or Livy. Livy wrote 142 books about Rome's history. People have found copies of 35 of Livy's books. Historians know there were 142 because other writers mention them.

CHAPTER 2

EARLY ROME

Between 2000 and 1000 BC, tribes of **nomads** from central Europe came to Italy. These nomads were known as the Latins.

The Latins settled on seven hills near the Tiber River in central Italy. The fertile land and warm climate allowed a long growing season. The Latins built villages and became farmers.

The Latins found other advantages to their new home near the Mediterranean Sea. Living close to two bodies of water was good for trade. Salt flats lay near the Tiber River. Latins traded salt with other people in the area.

According to ancient stories, some of the larger Latin settlements united in 753 BC. They formed a city-state called Rome.

nomad: a person who travels from place to place to find food and water

The Latins built settlements on the hills along the Tiber River.

The Etruscans built many buildings out of stone, including tombs like this one.

The Greeks and the Etruscans

While the Latins settled Rome, other groups occupied different parts of Italy. The Greeks, living in the south, were more advanced than the Latins. Greeks could read and write. As the Latins traded with the Greeks, they adopted parts of the Greek culture.

The Etruscans settled north of Rome. Some historians believe Etruscans came from western Asia. These people built stone buildings and canals to move water. They had a strong army. The Etruscans were good farmers and skillful traders. They became richer than the Roman farmers.

After Rome was formed, the strongest leader became king. The first kings of Rome were Latins. But in 616 BC, Etruscans took over Rome.

In about 509 BC, Romans decided they wanted a different government. They defeated the Etruscan king. Rome became a **republic**, and the people began to elect their own leaders.

a statue created by an Etruscan artist

republic: a form of government in which people elect their leaders

CHAPTER 3

A REPUBLIC FORMS

In the Roman republic, people were divided into different social classes. Noble landowners, called patricians, were the wealthy, long-time citizens of Rome. Other Roman citizens were plebeians. Some plebeians had money. They were farmers or soldiers. Other plebeians were poor.

Under the new republic, kings no longer ruled. Instead, the Senate became the ruling body that passed laws. Patricians served on the Senate. Each year, two patricians were elected to serve as consuls. Consuls led the Senate and commanded the military.

In around 494 BC, the plebeians demanded equal representation in government. Roman government changed again. Plebeians could become tribunes. Tribunes attended all Senate meetings. They could **veto** decisions they thought were unfair.

veto: to refuse consent

Members of the Senate met to discuss laws and conflicts.

FACT: Both patricians and plebeians could own slaves. Slaves were not citizens.

Civil War

Even though citizens voted for Rome's leaders, there were still problems. Some Romans tried to take control of the government in sneaky ways. Some army generals served in the Senate. They forced other senators to vote certain ways. Because of this corruption, the Roman Senate was weakened.

Julius Caesar leads an army into battle during the Roman civil war.

In 60 BC, three generals united to lead Rome. Pompey, Marcus Crassus, and Julius Caesar worked together for nearly five years. But after Crassus died in battle, Caesar and Pompey argued over who should rule Rome. Romans sided with either Caesar or Pompey. A civil war began. Caesar's army defeated Pompey's army. Pompey fled to Egypt and was killed. Julius Caesar took control of Rome.

Dictator Caesar

Julius Caesar made some big changes during his rule. He lowered taxes. He also changed the government. Caesar named himself **dictator**. Many people believed Caesar was trying to become king of Rome. When Caesar named himself Dictator for Life, citizens were worried. Some angry senators killed Caesar in 44 BC.

dictator: a person who has complete power to rule over a country

an ancient statue
of Julius Caesar

15

CHAPTER 4

THE ROMAN EMPIRE

After Caesar was killed, civil war erupted again in Rome. The war lasted for more than 10 years. Three generals joined forces to gain control. Later, they fought each other for power. Octavian, Caesar's grandnephew, defeated the others. The Senate recognized Octavian as Rome's ruler in 27 BC.

Octavian changed Rome's government once again. After nearly 500 years as a republic, Rome found itself ruled by an **emperor**. Octavian called himself First Citizen. Citizens called Octavian "Augustus," which means "holy."

ancient statue of
Emperor Augustus

Octavian rides in a parade through Rome after being made emperor.

Emperor Augustus did not lead the Senate.
Instead, he made himself a tribune. Tribunes
could veto any law the Senate made. Augustus
ruled as an emperor while acting as a tribune.

emperor: a man who rules a large territory

Being Emperor

During the Roman Empire, emperors were in charge of the government. People could not elect the emperor or other leaders. The government was similar to the early days when Rome had a king. But the emperor ruled over a much larger area of land. He served as the court and the source of law. He was also the military commander and the high priest. Although the Senate still existed, it had little power.

When emperors died, they passed the throne to their sons or other relatives. These family lines created dynasties. Each dynasty was a period of time when all the emperors came from one family.

Emperors had fancy lifestyles. Slaves did anything the ruler wanted.

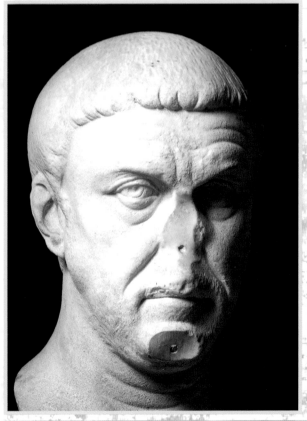

ancient statues of Diocletian (left) and Maximian (right)

A Divided Empire

Over time it became clear that Rome was too large for one emperor to rule. In AD 284, Emperor Diocletian divided Rome in half. He ruled the eastern half. His friend, Maximian, ruled the western half.

The Fall of the Empire

Rome's enemies saw how the empire's division weakened Rome. Germanic tribes, including the Ostrogoths, the Visigoths, and the Vandals, repeatedly attacked. The constant wars made the empire even weaker.

In AD 410, Visigoths from Germany sacked the city of Rome. They killed people, destroyed buildings, and took whatever they wanted.

The Western Roman Empire began to crumble. Tribes of Vandals conquered Africa. The Visigoths took parts of Spain. The Picts, people from Scotland and Northern Ireland, invaded England. When Emperor Romulus Augustus was dethroned in AD 476, the Western Roman Empire was nearly gone.

The Eastern Roman Empire continued for another 1,000 years. Emperors ruled from Constantinople, in present-day Turkey, until 1453. In that year, the Ottoman Turks brought the Eastern Roman Empire to an end.

The rest of the world was surprised and terrified when news spread that Rome had been destroyed by German tribes.

CHAPTER 5

A LASTING INFLUENCE

The people of ancient Rome lived full lives that still influence us today. The Romans became great builders. They combined cement with sand and gravel to make concrete. Using concrete, builders made walls with smooth sides. They designed round concrete roofs called domes.

Romans also built huge arenas and theaters. People attended gladiator fights in arenas called amphitheaters. Gladiators were slaves or prisoners trained to fight each other until one died. Early theaters were small, wooden buildings where actors performed plays. The theaters had no seats, so people had to stand.

Gladiators fought to the death in front of huge crowds.

Chariot racing was one of the most popular forms of entertainment in ancient Rome.

Circuses and Forums

Sports provided entertainment for Romans too. **Chariots** raced in an open racecourse called a circus. One of the most famous was the Circus Maximus. It was 1,800 feet (549 meters) long and 500 feet (152 meters) wide.

Most Roman cities had a forum. This large open area was usually in the center of town. The forum was a place to meet, shop, and listen to speakers.

chariot: a two-wheeled fighting platform that was usually pulled by horses

Spartacus (right center) died in the Battle of Silarus River, the final battle in the gladiators' fight for freedom.

Gladiators' War

Men who fought as gladiators were slaves, criminals, or prisoners of war. Gladiators trained at schools. At the schools, they were forced to learn how to fight with swords. Gladiators who survived three to five years of battle were freed.

In 73 BC, Spartacus and 75 other gladiators escaped. They stole weapons and hid on Mount Vesuvius. Thousands of slaves joined them. The Roman government sent soldiers to fight the slaves. Spartacus and his men held off the army for two years. In 71 BC, General Marcus Crassus, a leading Roman senator and general, led his army to defeat the gladiators.

Moving People and Water

Romans built paved roads so armies could easily move from one place to another. One of the first major roads in Rome was the Appian Way. It was built in 312 BC. The Appian Way was the main road to Campania, a region south of Rome.

The Romans built **aqueducts** to carry water from springs to cities. The Romans did not invent the aqueduct. They copied ideas developed by the Greeks and Babylonians. The size and length of Rome's aqueducts made them better. Eleven aqueducts brought water to Rome. Together they stretched for 260 miles (418 km).

aqueduct: a bridge built to carry water from a mountain into the valley

a Roman aqueduct in present-day France

FACT: Parts of some Roman aqueducts that were built in present-day Greece, Italy, Spain, and France still exist today.

Language

Ancient Romans spoke a language called Latin. Many modern-day languages, including French, Spanish, and Italian, came from Latin. Countries all over the world also use the Roman alphabet. Rome copied its alphabet from the Greeks. The English alphabet comes from the one the Romans used.

Government

Founders of the United States used lessons from Rome to help write the U.S. Constitution. They modeled the government after the Roman republic. The president, like a consul, serves for a specific amount of time. The U.S. Senate and U.S. House of Representatives are elected by the people.

The Roman Empire is remembered in our history, art, and architecture. Surviving monuments and buildings show the skill of Roman artists and builders. Countries model their governments after the Roman republic. Ancient Rome still influences cultures today.

Rome's influence can be seen in the design of the U.S. Capitol building.

Roman numerals are used in many places in our modern world, including books and clocks.

Roman Numerals

The Romans invented a number system that used only seven symbols. The symbols could be arranged to make any number. People still use Roman numerals today. Outlines for reports are often numbered in Roman numerals. Roman numerals also tell the number of kings with the same name. For example, England had eight kings named Henry. Each king had a Roman numeral after his name. The last one was King Henry VIII.

1	I
5	V
10	X
50	L
100	C
500	D
1000	M

TIMELINE

753 BC

According to legend, Romulus and Remus found Rome.

494 BC

The plebeians demand more representation in Roman government.

46 BC

Julius Caesar is named dictator. Two years later, senators in Rome murder him.

BC   700   500   100   40

509 BC

The Romans rebel against the Etruscan king and found the Roman Republic.

73–71 BC

Spartacus leads the Gladiators' War.

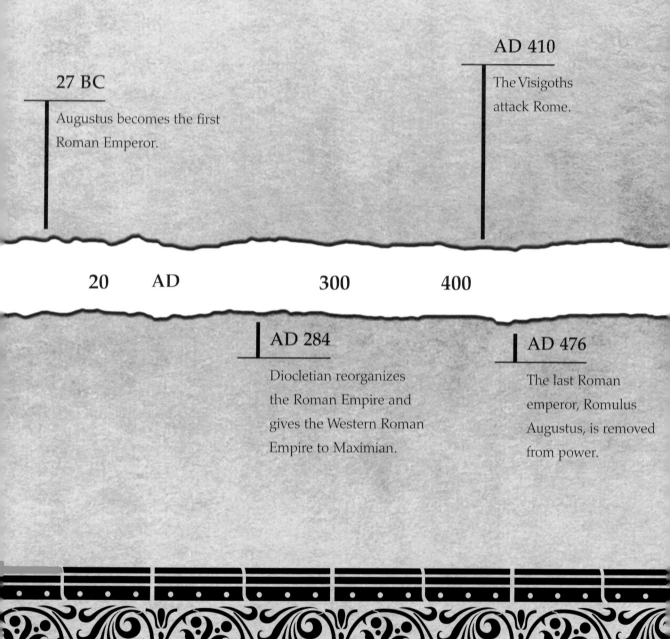

27 BC

Augustus becomes the first
Roman Emperor.

AD 410

The Visigoths
attack Rome.

20   AD   300   400

AD 284

Diocletian reorganizes
the Roman Empire and
gives the Western Roman
Empire to Maximian.

AD 476

The last Roman
emperor, Romulus
Augustus, is removed
from power.

GLOSSARY

aqueduct (AK-wuh-duhkt)—a large bridge built to carry water from a mountain into the valley

chariot (CHAYR-ee-uht)—a two-wheeled fighting platform used in ancient times that was usually pulled by a horse

city-state (SI-tee STAYT)—a self-governing community including a town and its surrounding territory

dictator (DIK-tay-tuhr)—a person who has complete power to rule over a country

emperor (EM-puhr-uhr)—a man who rules a large territory

empire (EM-pire)—a large territory ruled by a powerful leader

nomad (NOH-mad)—a person who travels from place to place to find food and water

Punic (PYOO-nihk)—the Latin word for Phoenician that was used to describe the wars between Rome and Carthage; the Phoenicians founded Carthage

republic (ree-PUHB-lik)—a form of government in which people elect their leaders

veto (VEE-toh)—to refuse consent or the power to forbid

READ MORE

Corrick, James A. *The Bloody, Rotten Roman Empire: The Disgusting Details about Life in Ancient Rome.* Disgusting History. Mankato, Minn.: Capstone Press, 2011.

Malam, John. *The Romans.* Dig It: History from Objects. New York: PowerKids Press, 2011.

Mara, Wil. *The Romans.* Technology of the Ancients. New York: Marshall Cavendish Benchmark, 2011.

Powell, Jillian. *The Romans.* The Gruesome Truth About. New York: Windmill Books, 2011.

INTERNET SITES

FactHound offers a safe, fun way to find Internet sites related to this book. All of the sites on FactHound have been researched by our staff.

Here's all you do:

Visit *www.facthound.com*

Type in this code: 9781429668323

Super-cool stuff!

Check out projects, games and lots more at
www.capstonekids.com

INDEX